Altar Servers'

Missal

Compiled by
THOMAS McMAHON

MCCRIMMONS
Great Wakering, Essex, England

First Published in United Kingdom in 1976 by
MAYHEW-McCRIMMON LTD

This edition published in United Kingdom in 2006 by
McCRIMMON PUBLISHING CO. LTD.
10-12 High Street, Great Wakering, Essex SS3 0EQ
www.mccrimmons.com

ISBN 0 85597 102 9   (10 digit ISBN)
ISBN 978-0-85597-102-1   (13 digit ISBN)
McCrimmon order ref: MB1029

Cum originali concordat	John P. Dewis
Nihil obstat	James Hawes, S.T.L.
Imprimatur	Christopher Creede, V.G.
Brentwood	15th April, 1976

Acknowledgements

English translation of the Order of the Mass. Copyright © 1969, 1971,
1976, International Committee on English in the Liturgy, Inc.
All rights reserved.

Edited by Kevin Grant
Cover design: Alan Hencher
Printed and bound by Thanet Press Ltd, Margate, Kent, UK   B/0A

Contents

Introduction

IT IS OFTEN SAID that our modern liturgy lacks any sense of mystery, and that it has now lost its feeling of being something sacred and holy. I do not think that this is true. If a Mass is celebrated with great care and preparation – if we are conscious of what we are about – then it can have a noble simplicity which lifts us up to God. We must always be anxious to show clearly, and give importance to, the four ways in which Christ is present during the Mass. First of all through the *People* gathered together: 'Where two or three are gathered together in my name there am I in the midst of them.' *(Matthew 18:20)* Then through the *Priest*, who presides through the name of the Bishop. He is the only one to act 'in persona Christi' (in the person of Christ). Christ is always present through his *Word*, which is why we surround it with marks of respect. Finally, Christ is present in the sacrificial victim on the altar whom we receive in Holy Communion through the mystery of the *Eucharist*.

One of the greatest means of emphasising all this is through altar servers. Obviously, the number of boys and girls depends on how many are available and on the size of the church. Servers add to the solemnity of an occasion, and make it possible to provide such things as a thurifer and acolytes at the principal Sunday Mass and so emphasise these four ways in which Christ is present.

In its document on the Liturgy, the Vatican Council said: 'Servers, readers, and members of the choir also exercise a genuine liturgical mystery. They ought therefore to discharge their office with a sincere piety and dignity demanded by so exalted a ministry'. This means that we must always be aware of the wonderful celebration in which we are taking part, and carry it out in the very best way that we can. This small missal has been produced with these two aims in mind.

I am most grateful to Fr. David Donnelly for kindly reading through the text, and for a number of corrections and suggestions that he has made.

Thomas McMahon

Prayers Before and After Serving

Go before us, O Lord,
in this our sacrifice of prayer and praise,
and grant that what we say and sing with our lips
we may believe in our hearts,
and that what we believe in our hearts
we may practice and show forth in our daily lives.
Through Christ our Lord. Amen.

AFTER

Bless, O Lord, our hearts and minds,
and grant that as we leave your house,
we may continue to be aware of your presence.
Through Christ our Lord. Amen.

The Church Year

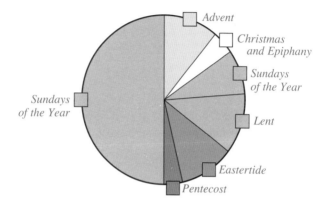

Advent

Christmas
and Epiphany

Sundays
of the Year

Lent

Eastertide

Pentecost

Sundays
of the Year

AS WE KNOW, the calendar year begins on the first day of
January. The Church's year, however, begins at the end of
November with the season we call Advent. This is because
the seasons of the Church take us through the life of Christ,
from before his birth to the time after his death. As in the
calendar year each season has its own beauty – the Spring
blossom and flowers; the warm Summer sunshine; the
Autumn colours and the beauty of a Winter landscape, so,
too, with the seasons of the Church. Each season has its
own message. Also, like the calendar year, with its ever
repeating cycle of birth (Spring) and death (Autumn), the
Church's year speaks of the birth, death and resurrection of
the ever living Christ.

Finally, as one season automatically leads us into another (Spring must naturally lead us into Summer), so, too, one season of the Church automatically leads us into the next. The theme of each Mass varies according to the season that we are in, and so this is why it is important to understand the meaning of each season so that we can grasp the message that is put across to us as the year unfolds.

Advent

This word comes from the Latin 'adventus' and means 'coming.' It has four Sundays, during which we prepare for the coming of the birth of Christ. The prophets who speak to us about the coming of Jesus during this period are Isaiah and John the Baptist. It is helpful to have an Advent wreath which, with its four candles, symbolises the four Sundays of Advent and welcomes the approach of the King of Light.

Christmas

This is the second greatest feast of the year and celebrates with great joy the birth of Christ. Like any birthday it is a time of great happiness, and we give and receive presents to show our joy and love. Jesus has come into our world to tell us about God and to show us the way to him.

Epiphany

This is a Greek word which means appearing or showing. Christ was born as an unknown child in a stable at Bethlehem, but through the three Wise Men who came to seek him, and went back to tell people about him, he was made known to the whole world. It is also known as the 'feast of lights' because of the star that guided them to Christ. We, too, must seek and follow Christ, 'the light of the world', and make him known to others.

Sundays of the Year

Easter Sunday is always on the Sunday after the first full moon following the Spring equinox on March 21st (the time when the sun crosses the equator). For this reason the date of Easter varies, and so there are a certain number of Sundays called 'Sundays of the Year' which fill in the time from Epiphany until Lent. They tell us about the beginning of the public life of Jesus.

Lent

This is the time of forty days beginning on Ash Wednesday and recalls the forty days Jesus spent praying and fasting in the desert. It is marked by sorrow for our sins and some form of penance, to show that we are really trying to live as Christ showed us. It ends with Holy Week, which includes Holy Thursday when we celebrate the Last Supper, which was the first Mass, and Good Friday when Christ died on the cross. During Lent we do not say the 'Glory to God in the highest' or the 'Alleluia', so as not to anticipate the joy of Easter.

Easter

This is the greatest feast of the whole year. It is even greater than Christmas, since the fulfilment of something is greater than its promise. On this day Jesus rose from the dead and promised that we, too, will rise one day. For this reason, we no longer see death as the end but as the beginning.

This is why the early christians changed the sabbath from Saturday to Sunday, and so in this sense every Sunday is a 'little Easter', and should be a day of great joy and hope.

Pentecost

This was a Jewish feast held on the fiftieth day after the Passover (which is what the word means). Forty days after Jesus rose from the dead he went back to the Father, and after ten more days, he sent down the Holy Spirit on Our Lady and the apostles. He sent the Holy Spirit in order to renew and strengthen them. The word 'Spirit' means breath or life. The receiving of the Spirit changed their lives and inspired the apostles to preach the Good News about Jesus. This is what happens when we receive the Holy Spirit.

Sundays of the Year

We have now retraced the life of Christ. The Church uses the other Sundays of the year that remain (about 34 in all) to put before us different aspects of his teaching. Each Sunday Mass will be given to one particular theme. We must listen carefully to the Lessons and Gospel, in order to understand what the message is.

The Vestments

MOST PEOPLE TODAY are very clothes conscious. They pay great attention to both style and colour. The kind of vestments worn in church, and their colour, have always had a special meaning. Besides the inner spiritual preparation there is also the outer physical one. The natural feeling that we ought to put on different clothing for divine worship was something that people had learnt long ago. There was always a special vestment for the presiding priest. It was not until city fashion changed to a new shorter costume that liturgical vestments came to be distinguished from ordinary dress. What the priest and server wear now still resembles the costume of ancient Rome.

Cassock

This word comes from the Italian word 'cassaca' and means great coat! It was the outer garb of priests and clerics. It used to be worn out of doors instead of a suit, but is now used as a garment for both priests and servers in church.

Surplice or Cotta

This goes over the server's cassock and is a smaller version of the Alb which the priest wears at Mass.

Amice

This is a linen cloth with two long tapes, which may be worn to cover the shoulders of the priest during Mass.

Alb

A long tunic in linen as worn in the 4th century. Its name comes from the Latin 'albus' meaning 'white'.

Cincture

A long piece of white cord which may be used to secure the Alb.

Stole

A very important vestment worn around the neck of the priest. It is thought to come from the silk scarf worn by orators. It is the distinctive mark of order worn by bishops, priests and deacons when cele-brating the sacraments. It also signifies the duty to preach the Word of God.

Chasuble

The word means literally a 'little house'. It is the outer garment which covers all the other vestments and its colour changes according to the feast or season.

COLOURS OF VESTMENTS

In worship, we are lifted up to God in various ways by what we say, and do, and hear. Another very important way is by what we can see. In this respect, colour always plays an important part in our lives. We choose colours carefully to reflect certain moods.

Purple

These vestments are worn for Advent and Lent, and express the mood of penance and preparation before a great feast.

White or Gold

These are worn on many important feasts. The colour is a sign of celebration and joy.

Red

This colour is used at Pentecost, to recall the fire of the Holy Spirit, Passion (Palm) Sunday, Good Friday and the feasts relating to the Holy Cross. It is used for feasts of martyrs, since they shed their blood for Christ.

Black

This may be worn for a funeral, although more usually today we wear purple or white, to express our belief in life after death and in the Resurrection.

Green

This is the colour you will see most often on a Sunday. This is because green is the colour of nature and of the new life which shoots forth in the Spring. This reminds us during the Church's year that we are always being given new life to nourish our spirit, as we listen to God's Word at Mass and receive Holy Communion. Green is the colour of hope, and the christian goes on his or her pilgrim way full of faith and hope.

The Sacred Vessels

Paten

A circular vessel resembling a flat plate on which the host rests during Mass.

Purificator

A folded piece of linen used to purify or cleanse the chalice.

Chalice

The sacred cup used at Mass to contain the Blood of Christ.

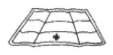

Corporal

This comes from the Latin 'corpus' meaning a 'body'. It is a square of linen cloth on which the paten containing the sacred host and the chalice are placed at Mass.

Pall

A linen-covered piece of stiff material which may be used to cover the chalice during Mass.

Chalice Veil

This is used to cover the chalice and is the same colour as the vestments of the day.

Burse

Although the burse is no longer in common use many churches retain it. It comes from the same word as purse, and has the same function of holding something. In this case it is used to hold the corporal.

Ciborium or Bowl

A vessel which contains the small hosts for the Communion of the people. In many places a deep bowl is used instead of a ciborium.

What to Prepare

IN THE CHURCH

Candles

A candle is not only useful in so far as it gives light, but it is a wonderful symbol of Christ who said: "I am the light of the world". For both these reasons candles have been used in worship since the very earliest times.

Lighting a candle can be very difficult, since, more often than not, you won't be able to see the top of the candle you are trying to light. If there are many candles, start with the highest (for obvious reasons!) starting near the centre of the altar and working outwards. One point worth remembering when carrying the candle lighter, is always to hold it with the flame rising upwards and not down, and then it won't flare up. If a candle proves difficult to light, quietly persevere or simply leave it.

Lectern

Make sure that the Lectionary is in place for the reader along with the Bidding Prayer. The reader should have had a chance to see them beforehand. The server may be required to hold the missal for the prayers at the beginning of Mass and again for the introduction and conclusion of the Bidding Prayers.

Credence Table

Here will be the Chalice, set up in the way shown on page 16. It is extremely important to see that the Tabernacle key is also out. The Lavabo cloth and bowl, and perhaps the bell, will also be on this table.

Servers' Books

Because most of the servers will be carrying things in the procession, it would be helpful to place the Cards or Missals for serving, and any hymn books, in their places beforehand.

Offertory Gifts

These may be on the table in the body of the Church and will consist of the the water and wine, and the Ciborium with the hosts for Holy Communion.

IN THE SACRISTY

Vestments

These should be laid out on the vestment press in the order in which the priests put them on. Since the Chasuble is put on last of all, it should be put out first. On top of this is put the Stole, then the Cincture, followed by the Alb, and last of all the Amice.

Missal

This should be marked and ready and placed in church, ready to bring up for the Opening Prayer.

Thurible

Prepare the charcoal and see that the Incense Boat is alongside it.

Acolytes

Have the candles and matches ready. Do hold them straight when they are lit, so that wax doesn't go all over the floor! Always remember to keep the outer hand on the middle of the candle and the other hand on the base.

Microphone and Lights

It is very important to see that these are switched on before Mass, so that you don't have to come rushing back and disrupt everything as soon as the Mass has begun.

AFTER MASS

Remain vested whilst you put out the candles and put away all the different things in the church and sacristy, or re-arrange them for the next Mass.

Manner of Serving

We all have our own part to play in the liturgy (which means, the form of service in church) and it is up to each one of us to understand fully what we are doing, and to carry it out as well as we can. The server must be aware of what he or she is doing and understand its inner meaning. Only in this way will we be able to bring the people to a fuller understanding of what it is we are involved in. The server has a very important part to play, since he or she is with the priest on the sanctuary the whole time, and can help more than anybody else to create the right atmosphere, or to detract from it! Thus the following points should be kept in mind.

1. The procession to and from the altar, and all actions on the altar, should be done slowly, with reverence, everybody keeping together, and with hands joined or clasped. The whole action must be calm and unhurried – conveying a feeling that one is aware of what one is about.

2. Bow or genuflect with care, so that it is a complete action, rather than something cut short.

3. Always stand up straight with both feet firmly on the floor – not leaning on one leg, or on anything else for that matter!

4. Any movement at all on the altar, apart from when you are actually serving, distracts people and draws their attention away from what is being said or done at that particular time. Therefore, no moving or talking on the side! Always look to where the action is: at the altar, lectern, or chair, and not at the people.

5. Mistakes easily happen. It is much better to disregard a mistake, if possible, than to draw attention to it.

6. Do arrive in good time and suitably dressed. Combed hair and appropriate clean footware all help the general presentation.

7. An atmosphere of quiet calm in the sacristy helps to dispose one for the ceremony in which one is about to take part.

Procession to the Altar

This usually forms up in the following order:

THURIFER (and Boat Boy)

ACOLYTE 1   CROSS   ACOLYTE 2

SERVERS

M.C.

BOOK-BEARER

DEACON

CONCELEBRANTS

CELEBRANT

At the Altar

Genuflect or bow together and move slowly to your places. Even when the tabernacle is present on the sanctuary, you only genuflect at the beginning and the end. This is because to turn attention to the real presence in the tabernacle during the Mass may direct attention away from the fact that Christ is also truly present within the celebration of Mass itself. We are celebrating the whole mystery of the Eucharist, sacrament and sacrifice, right from the beginning of the celebration.

Incense

Where this is used (see the explanation of its meaning on page 61) the thurifer comes to the priest and raises the lid of the thurible by means of the ring at the top of the centre chain. The thurifer then grasps the chain just above the lid with the right hand and raises the thurible to the level of the priest's hands. After the priest has put the incense on the charcoal (and blessed it) the thurifer lowers the thurible, closes the lid and passes the thurible to the priest with the right hand. You always receive it back in your left hand, since you then have your right hand free to keep it swinging gently.

Gospel Procession

Wherever possible, the reader of the Gospel should be accompanied by the thurifer and acolytes carrying lighted candles. This shows the importance of Christ and the honour due to him as he speaks to us through the Gospel. Incense is put in before the procession moves off. Do try and keep together, since this procession is very impressive when it is done well.

Procession with the Gifts

The bread and wine and the Offertory collection are brought up by the people. The procession may be led up the church by servers but in this simple procession of gifts neither the cross nor candles are carried.

Water and Wine

Bow to the priest as you take away the water and wine, and after the washing of hands.

Incense

This may be used again at this point, and comes just before the washing of hands. If you take the thurible to the sacristy, after incensing the people, wait until the 'Holy, holy, holy…' returning, so as not to distract the people during the Preface.

Bells

These may be rung at the most solemn moment of the Mass which is called the Consecration. Give a firm ring – neither too short nor too long – as the priest raises up the sacred host and again when he raises up the chalice.

Sign of Peace

This should be given with reverence, and joy and feeling, according to the custom of the local Church.

After Holy Communion

Keep very still during the silence and try to speak to Our Lord in your own words or say one or two of the prayers on page 53.

Procession from the Altar

Form up once again in the same order as you did for the entrance and move slowly down the aisle, keeping together.

The Mass

INTRODUCTORY RITES

Each of us shares in the Mass by being present. Though the priest leads the offering of the Eucharistic Sacrifice Christ desires each of us to share with him as fully as possible. The Church urges us to gather near the altar, to answer the responses, to join in the singing, even if we feel we cannot sing well, and to receive Holy Communion.

When the priest has reached the altar everyone makes the sign of the cross:

In the name of the Father, and of the Son, and of the Holy Spirit.

Amen.

The priest greets the people in one of the following ways, or in similar words:

1 The grace of our Lord Jesus Christ and the love of God and the fellowship of the Holy Spirit be with you all.
   And also with you.

---

2 The grace and peace of God our Father and the Lord Jesus Christ be with you.
   Blessed be God, the Father of our Lord Jesus Christ.
      And also with you.

---

3 The Lord be with you.
   And also with you.

The priest invites us to say we are sorry to God and to one another in one of the following ways, or in similar words:

26

1 My brothers and sisters,
   to prepare ourselves to celebrate the sacred mysteries,
   let us call to mind our sins.

After a brief silence, all say:
I confess to almighty God,
and to you, my brothers and sisters,
that I have sinned through my own fault
All strike their breast
in my thoughts and in my words,
in what I have done,
and in what I have failed to do;
and I ask blessed Mary, ever virgin,
all the angels and saints,
and you, my brothers and sisters,
to pray for me to the Lord our God.
May almighty God have mercy on us,
forgive us our sins,
and bring us to everlasting life.
Amen.
Lord, have mercy. **Lord, have mercy.**
Christ, have mercy. **Christ, have mercy.**
Lord, have mercy. **Lord, have mercy.**

Turn to the Gloria on page 29 except in Advent and Lent.
2 My brothers and sisters,
   to prepare ourselves to celebrate the sacred mysteries,
   let us call to mind our sins.

After a brief silence, the celebrant says:
Lord, we have sinned against you:

Lord, have mercy.
Lord, have mercy.
Lord, show us your mercy and love.
And grant us your salvation.
May almighty God have mercy on us,
forgive us our sins,
and bring us to everlasting life.
Amen.
Lord, have mercy. **Lord, have mercy.**
Christ, have mercy. **Christ, have mercy.**
Lord, have mercy. **Lord, have mercy.**

Turn to the Gloria on page 29 except in Advent and Lent.

3 My brothers and sisters,
   to prepare ourselves to celebrate the sacred mysteries,
   let us call to mind our sins.

After a brief silence the priest says the following, or uses
similar words. The people's response, however, remains the
same.

You were sent to heal the contrite:
Lord, have mercy.
Lord, have mercy.
You came to call sinners:
Christ, have mercy.
Christ, have mercy.
You plead for us at the right hand of the Father:
Lord, have mercy.
Lord, have mercy.

May almighty God have mercy on us,
forgive us our sins,
and bring us to everlasting life.
Amen.

THE GLORIA

This is a hymn written in the 5th century to express joy at
the birth of Christ.

Glory to God in the highest,
and peace to his people on earth.

Lord God, heavenly King,
almighty God and Father,
we worship you, we give you thanks,
we praise you for your glory.

Lord Jesus Christ, only Son of the Father,
Lord God, Lamb of God,
you take away the sin of the world:
have mercy on us;
you are seated at the right hand of the Father:
receive our prayer.

For you alone are the Holy One,
you alone are the Lord,
you alone are the Most High,
Jesus Christ,
with the Holy Spirit,
in the glory of God the Father. Amen.

THE OPENING PRAYER (The Collect)

This prayer 'collects' together our spiritual needs, asked for in our name by the priest. You bring the missal to the priest for this prayer. We all join in at the end by saying Amen.

LITURGY OF THE WORD

THE READINGS

Two readings from Scripture now follow, one from the Old Testament (which usually has a theme linking with the Gospel) and then a New Testament lesson. Listen carefully since it is God who speaks to us through his Word. A Psalm, which is an Old Testament poem, separates the two readings. At the end of each reading say **Thanks be to God.**

THE GOSPEL

At the principal Sunday Mass incense may be put in the thurible at this point and the acolytes get their candles to accompany the book of the Gospels. The word Gospel means 'Good News' and the reading is always about Christ, hence the marks of honour with which it is surrounded. At the end of the Gospel we say **Praise to you, Lord Jesus Christ.**

THE HOMILY

This follows the Readings and Gospel since now the priest explains their meaning to us.

CREED

Having listened to God's word we now state publicly the main beliefs of our faith.

We believe in one God,
the Father, the Almighty,
maker of heaven and earth,
of all that is, seen and unseen.

We believe in one Lord, Jesus Christ,
the only Son of God,
eternally begotten of the Father,
God from God, Light from Light,
true God from true God,
begotten, not made,
of one Being with the Father.
Through him all things were made.
For us men and for our salvation
he came down from heaven:
by the power of the Holy Spirit
he became incarnate from the Virgin Mary, and
was made man.

All bow during the
next three lines.

For our sake he was crucified under Pontius Pilate;
he suffered death and was buried.
On the third day he rose again
in accordance with the Scriptures;
he ascended into heaven
and is seated at the right hand of the Father.
He will come again in glory to judge the living and
the dead,
and his kingdom will have no end.

We believe in the Holy Spirit, the Lord, the giver of life,
who proceeds from the Father and the Son.
With the Father and the Son he is worshipped and
glorified.

He has spoken through the Prophets.
We believe in one holy catholic and apostolic Church.

We acknowledge one baptism for the forgiveness of sins.
We look for the resurrection of the dead,
and the life of the world to come. Amen.

Now come the Bidding Prayers or the Prayer of the Faithful. We offer our prayers for the Church, for the world and local needs. The petitions may end with the words Lord, hear us, and the response is **Lord, graciously hear us**.

It is usual for two or three people to represent the congregation by bringing the bread and wine to the altar. You may assist the priest in receiving these gifts – after which he will say these prayers.

LITURGY OF THE EUCHARIST

PREPARATION OF THE GIFTS

Blessed are you, Lord, God of all creation.
Through this goodness we have this bread to offer,
which earth has given and human hands have made.
It will become for us the bread of life.
Blessed be God for ever.

You then bring up the water and wine. The wine will later become the Blood of Christ and the water represents ourselves. This is a sign of the coming together of the human and the divine.

Blessed are you, Lord, God of all creation.

Through your goodness we have this wine to offer,
fruit of the vine and work of human hands.

It will become our spiritual drink.
Blessed be God for ever.
Lord God, we ask you to receive us and be pleased with
the sacrifice we offer you with humble and contrite hearts.

Incense may be used at this point.
The priest washes his hands, saying quietly:
Lord, wash away my iniquity;
cleanse me from my sin.
Pray, brethren, that my sacrifice and yours
may be acceptable to God the almighty Father.
May the Lord accept the sacrifice at your hands,
for the praise and glory of his name,
for our good, and the good of all his Church.

The priest says the Prayer over the Gifts and then begins the
Preface – a prayer of thanks and praise, changing with the
season or feast.
The Lord be with you.
And also with you.
Lift up your hearts.
We lift them up to the Lord.
Let us give thanks to the Lord our God.
It is right to give him thanks and praise.

The Preface follows. At the end everyone says or sings:
Holy, holy, holy Lord, God of power and might,
heaven and earth are full of your glory.
   Hosanna in the highest.

Blessed is he who comes in the name of the Lord.
  Hosanna in the highest.

Eucharistic Prayer 1 starts on this page.
Turn to
page 39 for Eucharistic Prayer 2,
page 42 for Eucharistic Prayer 3,
page 45 for Eucharistic Prayer 4.

The word 'Eucharist' comes from the Greek, meaning 'Thanksgiving'. It indicates we are going to do what Christ did, that is: 'taking bread he gave thanks'. The central point is the Consecration – our sacrifice of praise – when the bread and wine become the true body and blood of Jesus Christ.

EUCHARISTIC PRAYER 1

(The passages within the brackets may be omitted if the celebrant wishes.)

We come to you, Father,
with praise and thanksgiving,
through Jesus Christ your Son.

Through him we ask you to accept and bless
these gifts we offer you in sacrifice.
We offer them for your holy catholic Church,

watch over it, Lord, and guide it;
grant it peace and unity throughout the world.
We offer them for N. our Pope,
for N. our bishop,
and for all who hold and teach the catholic faith
that comes to us from the apostles.

Remember, Lord, your people,
especially those for whom we now pray, N. and N.
Remember all of us gathered here before you.
You know how firmly we believe in you
and dedicate ourselves to you.
We offer you this sacrifice of praise
for ourselves and those who are dear to us.
We pray to you, our living and true God,
for our well-being and redemption.
In union with the whole Church
we honour Mary,
the ever-virgin mother of Jesus Christ our Lord and God.
We honour Joseph, her husband,
the apostles and martyrs
Peter and Paul, Andrew,
(James, John, Thomas,
James, Philip,
Bartholomew, Matthew, Simon and Jude;
we honour Linus, Cletus, Clement, Sixtus,
Cornelius, Cyprian, Lawrence, Chrysogonus,
John and Paul, Cosmas and Damian)
and all the saints.

May their merits and prayers
gain us your constant help and protection.
(Through Christ our Lord. Amen.)

Father, accept this offering
from your whole family.
Grant us your peace in this life,
save us from final damnation,
and count us among those you have chosen.
(Through Christ our Lord. Amen.)

Bless and approve our offering;
make it acceptable to you,
an offering in spirit and in truth.
Let it become for us
the body and blood of Jesus Christ,
your only Son, our Lord.

The day before he suffered
he took bread in his sacred hands
and looking up to heaven,
to you, his almighty Father,
he gave you thanks and praise.
He broke the bread,
gave it to his disciples, and said:

Take this, all of you, and eat it:
this is my body which will be given up for you.

When supper was ended, he took the cup.
Again he gave you thanks and praise,
gave the cup to his disciples, and said:

Take this, all of you, and drink from it:
this is the cup of my blood,
the blood of the new and everlasting covenant.
It will be shed for you and for all men
so that sins may be forgiven.
Do this in memory of me.

Let us proclaim the mystery of faith:

1 **Christ has died,**
   Christ is risen,
   Christ will come again.

2 **Dying you destroyed our death,**
   rising you restored our life.
   Lord Jesus, come in glory.

3 **When we eat this bread and drink this cup,**
   we proclaim your death, Lord Jesus,
   until you come in glory.

4 **Lord, by your cross and resurrection**
   you have set us free.
   You are the Saviour of the world.

5 (for Ireland) **My Lord and my God.**

Father, we celebrate the memory of Christ, your Son.
We, your people and your ministers,
recall his passion,
his resurrection from the dead,

and his ascension into glory;
and from the many gifts you have given us
we offer to you, God of glory and majesty,
this holy and perfect sacrifice:
the bread of life
and the cup of eternal salvation.

Look with favour on these offerings
and accept them as you once accepted
the gifts of your servant Abel,
the sacrifice of Abraham, our father in faith,
and the bread and wine offered by your priest Melchisedech.

Almighty God,
we pray that your angel may take this sacrifice
to your altar in heaven.
Then, as we receive from this altar
the sacred body and blood of your Son,
let us be filled with every grace and blessing.
(Through Christ our Lord. Amen.)

Remember, Lord, those who have died
and have gone before us marked with the sign of faith,
especially those for whom we now pray, N. and N.
May these, and all who sleep in Christ,
find in your presence
light, happiness, and peace.
(Through Christ our Lord. Amen.)

For ourselves, too, we ask
some share in the fellowship of your apostles and martyrs,
with John the Baptist, Stephen, Matthias, Barnabas,

(Ignatius, Alexander, Marcellinus, Peter,
Felicity, Perpetua, Agatha, Lucy,
Agnes, Cecilia, Anastasia)
and all the saints.

Though we are sinners,
we trust in your mercy and love.
Do not consider what we truly deserve,
but grant us your forgiveness.

Through Christ our Lord
you give us all these gifts.
You fill them with life and goodness,
you bless them and make them holy.

Through him,
with him,
in him,
in the unity of the Holy Spirit,
all glory and honour is yours,
almighty Father,
for ever and ever.
Amen.

Continue on page 50.

EUCHARISTIC PRAYER 2

Lord, you are holy indeed,
the fountain of all holiness.
Let your Spirit come upon these gifts to make them holy,
so that they may become for us
the body and blood of our Lord, Jesus Christ.

Before he was given up to death,
a death he freely accepted,
he took bread and gave you thanks.
He broke the bread,
gave it to his disciples, and said:

> Take this, all of you, and eat it:
> this is my body which will be given up for you.

When supper was ended, he took the cup.
Again he gave you thanks and praise,
gave the cup to his disciples, and said:

> Take this, all of you, and drink from it:
> this is the cup of my blood,
> the blood of the new and everlasting covenant.
> It will be shed for you and for all men
> so that sins may be forgiven.
> Do this in memory of me.

Let us proclaim the mystery of faith:

1 **Christ has died,**
  Christ is risen,
  Christ will come again.

2 **Dying you destroyed our death,**
  rising you restored our life.
  Lord Jesus, come in glory.

3 **When we eat this bread and drink this cup,**
  we proclaim your death, Lord Jesus,
  until you come in glory.

4 Lord, by your cross and resurrection
 you have set us free.
 You are the Saviour of the world.

5 (for Ireland) **My Lord and my God.**

In memory of his death and resurrection,
we offer you, Father, this life-giving bread,
this saving cup.
We thank you for counting us worthy
to stand in your presence and serve you.
May all of us who share in the body and blood of Christ
he brought together in unity by the Holy Spirit.

Lord, remember your Church throughout the world;
make us grow in love,
together with N. our Pope,
N. our bishop, and all the clergy.

Remember our brothers and sisters
who have gone to their rest
in the hope of rising again;
bring them and all the departed
into the light of your presence.
Have mercy on us all;
make us worthy to share eternal life
with Mary, the virgin Mother of God,
with the apostles, and with all the saints
who have done your will throughout the ages.
May we praise you in union with them,
and give you glory
through your Son, Jesus Christ.

Through him,
with him,
in him,
in the unity of the Holy Spirit,
all glory and honour is yours,
almighty Father,
for ever and ever.
Amen.   Continue on page 50.

EUCHARISTIC PRAYER 3

Father, you are holy indeed,
and all creation rightly gives you praise.
All life, all holiness comes from you
through your Son, Jesus Christ our Lord,
by the working of the Holy Spirit.
From age to age you gather a people to yourself,
so that from east to west
a perfect offering may be made
to the glory of your name.
And so Father, we bring you these gifts.
We ask you to make them holy by the power of your Spirit,
that they may become the body and blood
of your Son, our Lord Jesus Christ,
at whose command we celebrate this eucharist.
On the night he was betrayed,
he took bread and gave you thanks and praise.
He broke the bread, gave it to his disciples, and said:

Take this, all of you, and eat it:
this is my body which will be given up for you.

When supper was ended, he took the cup.
Again he gave you thanks and praise,
gave the cup to his disciples, and said:

Take this, all of you, and drink from it:
this is the cup of my blood,
the blood of the new and everlasting covenant.
It will be shed for you and for all men
so that sins may be forgiven.
Do this in memory of me.

Let us proclaim the mystery of faith:

1 **Christ has died,**
   Christ is risen,
   Christ will come again.

2 **Dying you destroyed our death,**
   rising you restored our life.
   Lord Jesus, come in glory.

3 **When we eat this bread and drink this cup,**
   we proclaim your death, Lord Jesus,
   until you come in glory.

4 **Lord, by your cross and resurrection**
   you have set us free.
   You are the Saviour of the world.

5 (for Ireland) **My Lord and my God.**

Father, calling to mind the death your Son endured for our
   salvation,

his glorious resurrection and ascension into heaven,
and ready to greet him when he comes again,
we offer you in thanksgiving this holy and living sacrifice
.
Look with favour on your Church's offering,
and see the Victim whose death has reconciled us to
    yourself.
Grant that we, who are nourished by his body and blood,
may be filled with his Holy Spirit,
and become one body, one spirit in Christ.

May he make us an everlasting gift to you
and enable us to share in the inheritance of your saints,
with Mary, the virgin Mother of God;
with the apostles, the martyrs,
(Saint N. the patron saint or saint of the day) and all
    your saints,
on whose constant intercession we rely for help.

Lord, may this sacrifice,
which has made our peace with you,
advance the peace and salvation of all the world.
Strengthen in faith and love your pilgrim Church on earth;
your servant, Pope N., our bishop N.,
and all the bishops,
with the clergy and the entire people your Son has gained
    for you.
Father, hear the prayers of the family you have gathered
    here before you.
In mercy and love unite all your children
wherever they may be.

Welcome into your kingdom our departed brothers and
   sisters,
and all who have left this world in your friendship.
We hope to enjoy for ever the vision of you glory,
through Christ our Lord, from whom all good things come.
Through him,
with him,
in him,
in the unity of the Holy Spirit,
all glory and honour is yours,
almighty Father,
for ever and ever.
Amen.   Continue on page 50.

EUCHARISTIC PRAYER 4

When this Eucharistic Prayer is used, the following Preface
is always said.

The Lord be with you.
And also with you.

Lift up your hearts.
We lift them up to the Lord.

Let us give thanks to the Lord our God.
It is right to give him thanks and praise.

Father in heaven,
it is right that we should give you thanks and glory:
you alone are God, living and true.
Through all eternity you live in unapproachable light.

Source of life and goodness, you have created all things,
to fill your creatures with every blessing
and lead all men to the joyful vision of your light.
Countless hosts of angels stand before you to do your will;
they look upon your splendour
and praise you, night and day.
United with them,
and in the name of every creature under heaven,
we too praise your glory as we sing (say):

Holy, holy, holy Lord, God of power and might,
heaven and earth are full of your glory.
   Hosanna in the highest.
Blessed is he who comes in the name of the Lord.
   Hosanna in the highest.

Father, we acknowledge your greatness:
all your actions show your wisdom and love.
You formed man in your own likeness
and set him over the whole world
to serve you, his creator,
and to rule over all creatures.
Even when he disobeyed you and lost your friendship
you did not abandon him to the power of death,
but helped all men to seek and find you.
Again and again you offered a covenant to man,
and through the prophets taught him to hope for salvation.
Father, you so loved the world
that in the fullness of time you sent your only Son to be
   our Saviour.

He was conceived through the power of the Holy Spirit,
and born of the Virgin Mary,
a man like us in all things but sin.
To the poor he proclaimed the good news of salvation,
to prisoners, freedom,
and to those in sorrow, joy.
In fulfilment of your will
he gave himself up to death;
but by rising from the dead,
he destroyed death and restored life.
And that we might live no longer for ourselves but for him,
he sent the Holy Spirit from you, Father,
as his first gift to those who believe,
to complete his work on earth
and bring us the fullness of grace.
Father, may this Holy Spirit sanctify these offerings.
Let them become the body and blood of Jesus Christ our
    Lord
as we celebrate the great mystery
which he left us as an everlasting covenant.
He always loved those who were his own in the world.
When the time came for him to be glorified by you, his
    heavenly Father,
he showed the depth of his love.
While they were at supper,
he took bread, said the blessing, broke the bread,
and gave it to his disciples, saying:

Take this, all of you, and eat it:
this is my body which will be given up for you.

In the same way, he took the cup, filled with wine.
He gave you thanks, and giving the cup to his disciples, said:

Take this, all of you, and drink from it:
this is the cup of my blood,
the blood of the new and everlasting covenant.
It will be shed for you and for all men
so that sins may be forgiven.
Do this in memory of me.

Let us proclaim the mystery of the faith:

1 **Christ has died,**
Christ is risen,
Christ will come again.

2 **Dying you destroyed our death,**
rising you restored our life.
Lord Jesus, come in glory.

3 **When we eat this bread and drink this cup,**
we proclaim your death, Lord Jesus,
until you come in glory.

4 **Lord, by your cross and resurrection**
you have set us free.
You are the Saviour of the world.

5 **(for Ireland) My Lord and my God.**

Father, we now celebrate this memorial of our redemption.
We recall Christ's death, his descent among the dead,
his resurrection, and his ascension to your right hand;

and, looking forward to his coming in glory,
we offer you his body and blood,
the acceptable sacrifice

which brings salvation to the whole world.
Lord, look upon this sacrifice which you have given to
    your Church;
and by your Holy Spirit, gather all who share this bread
    and wine*
into the one body of Christ, a living sacrifice of praise.

Lord, remember those for whom we offer this sacrifice,
especially N. our Pope,
N. our bishop, and bishops and clergy everywhere.
Remember those who take part in this offering,
those here present and all your people,
and all who seek you with a sincere heart.
Remember those who have died in the peace of Christ
and all the dead whose faith is known to you alone.
Father, in your mercy grant also to us, your children,
to enter into our heavenly inheritance
in the company of the Virgin Mary, the Mother of God,
and your apostles and saints.
Then, in your kingdom, freed from the corruption of sin
    and death,
we shall sing your glory with every creature through
    Christ our Lord,
through whom you give us everything that is good.
Through him,
with him,

in him,
in the unity of the Holy Spirit,
all glory and honour is yours,
* (alternative version in England and Wales) this one bread
and one cup

almighty Father,
for ever and ever.
Amen.

COMMUNION RITE

We say the great prayer of Jesus together as one family in
Christ. The priest uses these words or similar.

Let us pray with confidence to the Father
in the words our Saviour gave us:

Our Father...
Deliver us, Lord, from every evil,
and grant us peace in our day.
In your mercy keep us free from sin
and protect us from all anxiety
as we wait in joyful hope
for the coming of our Saviour, Jesus Christ.

**For the kingdom, the power, and the glory are yours,
    now and for ever.**

Lord Jesus Christ, you said to your apostles:
I leave you peace, my peace I give you.
Look not on our sins, but on the faith of your Church,
and grant us the peace and unity of your kingdom
where you live for ever and ever.
Amen.

The peace of the Lord be with you always.
And also with you.
Then the priest may add:
Let us offer each other the sign of peace.

Now we acknowledge publicly that we want to be at peace
with one another. The Church suggests we show this by a
sign of peace.

May this mingling of the body and blood of our Lord Jesus
Christ bring eternal life to us who receive it.

Lamb of God, you take away the sins of the world:
  have mercy on us.
Lamb of God, you take away the sins of the world:
  have mercy on us.
Lamb of God, you take away the sins of the world:
  grant us peace.

Lord Jesus Christ, Son of the living God, by the will of the
Father and the work of the Holy Spirit your death brought
life to the world. By your holy body and blood free me from
all my sins and from every evil. Keep me faithful to your
teaching, and never let me be parted from you.

or

Lord Jesus Christ, with faith in you love and mercy I eat
your body and drink your blood. Let it not bring me
condemnation, but health in mind and body.

This is the Lamb of God
who takes away the sins of the world.
Happy are those who are called to his supper.

Lord, I am not worthy to receive you,
but only say the word and I shall be healed.

We become ever more closely one with Christ and with each other by sharing the breaking of bread, receiving together the body and blood of Jesus Christ in Holy Communion.

This time can often seem very long for prayers, especially when there are large numbers at Communion. Do resist the temptation to distract one another! Instead, talk to God in your own words about the week that is over, or the week that is just beginning, or something the priest spoke of during the sermon. There are also some prayers on page 53. When the priest has given out Holy Communion, he will then need the water, to purify the chalice. Then take the chalice and ciborium to the credence table. After the silence the priest will need the Missal for the Prayer after Communion and after that the notice book.

PRAYER AFTER COMMUNION

The Lord be with you.
And also with you.

The priest blesses the people. On certain occasions he may use a more solemn blessing or prayer over the people.

May almighty God bless you,
the Father, and the Son, and the Holy Spirit.
Amen.

The priest dismisses the people with one of the following:

The Mass is ended, go in peace.
Thanks be to God.

Go in the peace of Christ.
Thanks be to God.

Go in peace to love and serve the Lord.
Thanks be to God.

We have worshipped together in the Eucharist. When Mass is ended we should go out joyfully to the world, continuing to greet each other in joy and service, for we go as Christ's messengers to the world he has made in which we live.

Some prayers of thanksgiving can be found in the following pages.

Prayers

Prayer of offering

Lord Jesus,
  I give you my hands to do your work.
  I give you my feet to go your way.
  I give you my eyes to see as you do.
  I give you my tongue to speak your words.
  I give you my mind that you may think in me.
  I give you my spirit that you may pray in me.

Above all
> I give you my heart that you may love in me,
> your Father, and all mankind.
> I give you my whole self that you may grow in me,
> so that it is you, Lord Jesus,
> who live and work and pray in me.

God be in my head, and in my understanding,
God be in mine eyes, and in my looking,
God be in my mouth, and in my speaking,
God be in my heart, and in my thinking,
God be at my end, and at my departing.

Book of hours (1514)

To grow nearer to God

> Day by day,
> O Lord,
> three things I pray:
> to see thee more clearly,
> love thee more dearly,
> follow thee more nearly,
> day by day. Amen.

St Richard of Chichester (d.1283)

Prayer after Communion

Lord, may the Sacrament we have taken revive us with food for the Spirit and support us with bodily help. Through Christ our Lord.

Roman Missal

For Christian witness

Guide me, teach me, strengthen me, till I become such a person as thou wouldst have me be, pure and gentle, truthful and high-minded, brave and able, courteous and generous, dutiful and useful.

Charles Kingsley (1819-1875)

For ourselves and other people

> I hand over to your care, Lord,
> my soul and body,
> my mind and thoughts,
> my prayers and my hopes,
> my health and my work,
> my life and my death,
> my parents and my family,
> my friends and my neighbours,
> my country and all men,
> today
> and always.

Lancelot Andrews (1555-1626)

Love of God

Lord Jesus, you have taught us that love is the fulfilling of the law. Teach us now what love really is, how much it costs, how far it leads, how deep it digs into our selfish selves. Then give us the courage and the generosity to accept what this means today and tomorrow and in the whole future way of our lives.

Michael Hollings

In time of temptation

Help me, Lord, or I shall perish. Lord Jesus, stiller of storms, bring peace to my soul. Lord Jesus, I want to please thee rather than to sin, and if I do not feel that I want to please thee, give me the grace to want to please thee. I *want* to want to please thee… and I do not want to sin.

Hubert van Zeller O.S.B.

Act of contrition

O my God, because you are so good, I am very sorry that I have sinned against you and by the help of your grace I will try not to sin again.

Jesus, I love you because you love me. I am sorry I have been selfish and let you down. Help me to answer your love with mine.

Michael Hollings

Joy in forgiveness

Happy the man whose offence is forgiven,
whose sin is remitted.
O happy the man to whom the Lord
imputes no guilt,
in whose spirit is no guile.

Psalm 31

Before study

O God, who hast ordained that whatever is to be desired should be sought by labour, and who, by thy blessing, bringest honest labour to good effect, look with mercy upon my studies and endeavours. Grant me, O Lord, only what is lawful and right, and afford me calmness of mind, and steadiness of purpose, so that I may so do thy will in this short life, as to obtain happiness in the world to come, for the sake of Jesus Christ our Lord.

Samuel Johnson (1709-1784)

In coldness of heart

O my sweet Saviour Christ, which in thine undeserved love towards mankind, so kindly wouldst suffer the painful death of the cross, suffer me not to be cold nor lukewarm in love again towards thee.

St. Thomas More (1478-1535)

For sharing

Make us worthy, Lord, to serve our fellow men throughout the world who live and die in poverty and hunger. Give them through our hands this day their daily bread, and by our understanding love, give peace and joy.

Mother Teresa of Calcutta

In worry

O Lord, we know we very often worry about things that may never happen. Help us to live one day at a time, and to live it for you, for your name's sake.

Beryl Bye

For perseverance

O Lord, support us all the day long until the shades lengthen and the evening comes, and the busy world is hushed, and the fever of life is over, and our work is done. Then, Lord, in thy mercy, grant us a safe lodging, a holy rest, and peace at the last. Amen.

John Henry Newman (1801-1890)

Love for others

Lord, make me an instrument of your peace:
    where there is hatred let me sow love,
    where there is injury let me sow pardon,
    where there is doubt let me sow faith,
    where there is despair let me give hope,
    where there is darkness let me give light,
    where there is sadness let me give joy.
O Divine Master, grant that I may
    not try to be comforted but to comfort,
    not try to be understood but to understand,
    not try to be loved but to love.
Because it is in giving that we receive,
    it is in forgiving that we are forgiven,
    and it is in dying that we are born to eternal life.

St. Francis of Assisi (1182-1226)

Evening prayer

Receive, O Lord, our prayers and works of this day, and grant us rest, so that we may serve you with renewed fervour.

Save us, O Lord, while waking, and guard us while sleeping, that when we wake, we may watch with Christ, and when we sleep, we may rest in peace.

Roman Breviary

Joy in thanksgiving

Cry out with joy to the Lord, all the earth.
Serve the Lord with gladness.
Come before him singing with joy.
Know that he, the Lord, is God.
He made us, we belong to him,
we are his people, the sheep of his flock.
Go within his gates giving thanks.
Enter his courts with songs of praise.
Give thanks to him and bless his name.
Indeed, how good is the Lord,
eternal his merciful love.
He is faithful from age to age.

Psalm 99

Benediction

This service takes its name from 'benedicere' which means 'to bless'. In the middle of the service the priest blesses us with the consecrated host.

Cope

A full vestment in the shape of a cloak and worn by the priest at Benediction.

Humeral Veil

Garment placed around the shoulders of the priest before he gives the blessing.

Monstrance

This word comes from 'Monstrare' which means 'to show'. It is the vessel in which the priest puts the consecrated host, so that it may be seen by all the people.

Thurible

This is used to contain the burning charcoal on which the incense is put. Incense has always been used since early times to do honour to people and things. For this reason we incense the altar, Gospel book, bread and wine, and people at Mass. At Benediction we incense the consecrated host.

Incense Boat

So called because it is the shape of a boat, and is used to hold the incense.

The following hymn may be sung. The priest then puts incense in the thurible and incenses the Blessed Sacrament.

O salutaris hostia,
quae caeli pandis ostium;
bella premunt hostilia,
da robur, fer auxilium.

Uni Trinoque Domino
sit sempiterna gloria,
qui vitam sine termino
nobis donet in patria.
Amen.

or

O saving victim, opening wide
the gate of heaven to man below;
our foes press on from every side;
your aid supply, your strength bestow.

To your great name be endless praise,
immortal Godhead, one in three;
O grant us endless length of days
in our true native land with thee. Amen.

Prayers, songs, readings and silence may now follow. Then everybody sings this hymn. After the first verse the priest puts incense in the thurible and incenses the Blessed Sacrament.

Tantum ergo Sacramentum
veneremur cernui:
et antiquum documentum
novo cedat ritui:
praestet fides supplementum
sensuum defectui.

Genitori, Genitoque
laus et jubilatio.
Salus, honor, virtus quoque
sit et benedictio;
procedenti ab utroque
compar sit laudatio. Amen.

or

Therefore we, before him bending,
this great Sacrament revere;
types and shadows have their ending,
for the newer rite is here;
faith our outward sense befriending,
makes the inward vision clear.

Glory let us give, and blessing
to the Father and the Son;
honour, might, and praise addressing,
while eternal ages run;
ever too his love confessing,
who, from both, with both is one. Amen.

Oremus. Deus, qui nobis, sub sacramento mirabili passionis
tuae memoriam reliquisti, tribue, quaesumus; ita nos

Corporis et Sanguinis tui sacra mysteria venerari, ut redemptionis tuae fructum in nobis iugiter sentiamus. Qui vivis et regnas in saecula saeculorum. **Amen.**

or

Let us pray.
Lord Jesus Christ,
you gave us the eucharist
as the memorial of your suffering and death.
May our worship of this sacrament of your body and blood
help us to experience the salvation you won for us
and the peace of the kingdom
where you live with the Father and the Holy Spirit,
one God, for ever and ever. **Amen.**

Now, bowing down in adoration, receive the benediction with the most Holy Sacrament. The server rings the bell and incenses the Blessed Sacrament.

The Divine Praises

Blessed be God.
Blessed be his holy Name.
Blessed be Jesus Christ, true God and true Man.
Blessed be the Name of Jesus.
Blessed be his most Sacred Heart.
Blessed be his most Precious Blood.
Blessed be Jesus in the most holy Sacrament of the Altar.
Blessed be the Holy Spirit, the Paraclete.
Blessed be the great Mother of God, Mary most holy.
Blessed be her holy and immaculate Conception.

Blessed be her glorious Assumption.
Blessed be the name of Mary, Virgin and Mother.
Blessed be Saint Joseph, her spouse most chaste.
Blessed be God in his Angels and his Saints.

While the priest replaces the Blessed Sacrament in the tabernacle, the following Psalm may be sung:

Adoremus in aeternum sanctissimum Sacramentum.
Laudate Dominum, omnes gentes,
laudate eum omnes populi.
Quoniam confirmata est super nos misericordia ejus;
et veritas Domini manet in aeternum.
Gloria Patri, et Filio,
et Spiritui Sancto.
Sicut erat in principio, et nunc, et semper,
et in saecula saeculorum. Amen.
Adoremus in aeternum sanctissimum Sacramentum.

or

Let us adore for ever the most holy Sacrament.
O praise the Lord, all you nations;
praise him, all you people.
For his mercy is confirmed upon us;
and the truth of the Lord remains for ever.

Glory be to the Father, and to the Son,
and to the Holy Spirit.
As it was in the beginning, is now,
and ever shall be, world without end. Amen.
Let us adore for ever the most holy Sacrament.

Weddings

Preparing the Church

Two kneelers and chairs will be required in front of the altar for the bride and groom. Also a small tray on which to place the wedding rings while they are being blessed.

The Nuptial Mass

If it is customary in your parish, you may meet the bride and groom at the door with the priest and go slowly in procession up the aisle. The Nuptial Mass is the same as any other Mass, with these three differences.

1. The wedding itself will take place after the homily.

2. A special blessing will be given to the newly married couple both after the Our Father, and following the Prayer after Communion, at the end of Mass.

3. There will be the signing of the register at some suitable moment.

Funerals

Preparing the Church

Make sure there is plenty of room in the front of the church for the coffin, allowing room for those who are carrying it to turn round, and for people to come up to Holy Communion during Mass.

The Pall and other Symbols

This is a large cloth which may be used to cover the coffin. Other symbols may be placed on the coffin, such as a crucifix and bible.

Candles

It is customary to place the Paschal candle near the coffin. This expresses our belief that death means a sharing in the new life and light of the Risen Christ. A separate table may be placed nearby for Mass cards.

Holy Water

This will be used during the service to remind us that the person who died shared in the life of Christ through the water of baptism.

Incense

This may be used as a mark of honour, and in the belief that the person who has died will one day share in the resurrection from the dead.

The Requiem Mass

This is like any other Mass until near the end. Following the Prayer after Communion (there is no blessing or dismissal), the priest says the prayers of Final Commendation. It is at this point he will need the holy water and incense, when they are used.